PRAISE
and
WORSHIP

A Key to Victory

SHARON DAUGHERTY

Sharon Daugherty
Victory Christian Center, Inc.
7700 South Lewis Avenue
Tulsa, Oklahoma 74136-7700 U.S.A.
www.victory.com

Published by Insight International, Inc.
contact@freshword.com
www.freshword.com
918-493-1718

ISBN: 978-1-943361-63-2
E-Book ISBN: 978-1-943361-64-9

Library of Congress Control Number: 2019914376

Printed in the United States of America.

CONTENTS

INTRODUCTION

Have you ever felt overwhelmed in life by circumstances around you that look impossible? The Bible gives many accounts of people who felt this way. We have to remember that we live in a fallen world because of Adam and Eve's sin. Because of sin, all of creation was negatively affected and continues to be today. The door was opened to the devil to bring havoc into the world at that time.

Realizing that there is a spiritual battle that has been going on for ages, there are reasons behind wars, strife, division, sickness, disease, pain, suffering, hardships, and other difficulties in the world in which we live. We have an enemy named Satan (also known as Lucifer or the devil) who wants to defeat us.

The Bible gives us insight on how to overcome in this world through our relationship with Jesus Christ and the Word of God, prayer, faith, and praise and worship to God.

In Acts 16, Paul and Silas had been thrown in prison and placed in chains. It was the midnight hour, the darkest hour, and instead of crying and complaining to each other, they began to sing praise to God. They sang loud enough that the other prisoners heard them. Suddenly, there was an earthquake that shook the prison. Chains fell off the prisoners and doors were opened. The prison keeper started to take his life thinking that the prisoners had all escaped, but Paul said, "**Do yourself no harm, for we are all here**" (v. 28).

Obviously, Paul had been preaching the Gospel in the prison while in chains, because the prison keeper asked, "**What must I do to be saved?**" (v. 30). Paul not only led him to the Lord, but he went and preached to his whole household and led them to the Lord.

Notice that their singing praise to God shook up things, causing chains of bondage to fall off, opening the door for the Gospel to be preached and for many to be saved.

When we learn to use the key of praising God, He can move in supernatural ways. We might not see everything changed at once, but our attitude changes. Faith rises in our hearts to believe. God begins to work in unusual ways, and we are able to hear Him give us direction. He shows us how to come out of whatever we are walking through.

In order to understand the key for breakthrough in praise and worship, we need to go back and understand how praise and worship began.

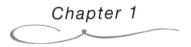

Chapter 1

THE ORIGIN OF PRAISE AND WORSHIP

Where did praise and worship begin? The answer to that question is in Heaven. The Host of Heaven worshipped God.

You alone are the Lord; You have made heaven, the heaven of heavens with all their host, the earth and everything on it, the seas and all that are in them, and You preserve them all. <u>**The Host of heaven worships You.**</u>

Nehemiah 9:6

(Also see Hebrews 1:5-6; Revelation 5:11-12.)

The prophet Ezekiel had supernatural visions, and he heard the voice of God speaking to him to write down what he was seeing and hearing from God. Ezekiel saw in a vision what had happened in Heaven.

Moreover the word of the Lord came to me, saying,

"Son of man, take up a lamentation for the king of Tyre, and say to him 'Thus says the Lord God: "You were the seal of perfection, full of wisdom and perfect in beauty.

You were in Eden, the garden of God; every precious stone was your covering: the sardius, topaz, and diamond, beryl, onyx, and jasper, sapphire, turquoise, and emerald with gold. The workmanship of your <u>timbrels</u> and <u>pipes</u> was prepared for you on the day you were created.

"You were the anointed cherub who covers; I established you; you were on the holy mountain of God; you walked back and forth in the midst of fiery stones.

You were perfect in your ways from the day you were created, till iniquity was found in you.

"By the <u>abundance</u> of your <u>trading*</u> you became filled with violence within, and you sinned; therefore I cast you as a profane thing out of the mountain of God; and I destroyed you, O covering cherub, from the midst of the fiery stones.

"Your heart was lifted up because of your beauty; you corrupted your wisdom for the sake of your splendor; I cast you to the ground, I laid you before kings (spirit kings as also seen in Daniel 10:13), **that they might gaze at you.**

"You defiled your sanctuaries by the multitude of your iniquities, by the iniquity of your trading* ... (In Hebrew the word trading is *"rekullah."* "Rekullah" refers to Lucifer walking up and down, slandering God to His subjects, attempting to win them over to himself *(Dake's Annotated Reference Bible).*

... Therefore I brought fire from your midst; it devoured you. . . .""""

Ezekiel 28:11-18

Theologians agree that this scripture is not speaking about an earthly king but about a spiritual king. (See also Daniel 10:13-14.) Ezekiel states that he was perfect in beauty and full of wisdom. He had been in the Garden of Eden. The only intelligent being in the Garden besides Adam and Eve was Satan who came in the form of a serpent. (Realize that a spirit can take on various forms.) Ezekiel goes on to say that in Heaven he was amazing to look at, covered with all types of jewels, plus he had instruments within his being. He was a full band within himself as he led worship in Heaven before the throne of God.

According to *Dake's Annotated Reference Bible*, the Hebrew word for "timbrels" is *"toph,"* which means tambourine, drums, tom toms, and percussion. (See also Psalm 150:5.)

Also according to Dake, the Hebrew word for "pipes" is *"hegeb,"* meaning a tubular hollow instrument. It can be made of metal, animal horn, or wood, such as flutes, pipes, horns, etc. (Also see Psalm 150:3.)

Lucifer (Satan) was the worship leader in Heaven, standing before the throne of God, leading angels in their worship to God. God had created the angels. They worshipped God day and night. Lucifer began to want their worship, and he wanted God's position of authority. He believed everything revolved around him anyway. This has been the downfall of other worship leaders on earth who have felt that their worship was the reason the church grew. It's called pride.

Another reference to Lucifer in Heaven is from the prophet Isaiah who saw a vision in the spirit and wrote the following words:

> "How you are fallen from heaven, O Lucifer, son of the morning! How you are cut down to the ground, you who weakened the nations!
>
> "For you have said in your heart: 'I will ascend into heaven, I will exalt my throne above

the stars of God; I will also sit on the mount of the congregation on the farthest sides of the north;

"'I will ascend above the heights of the clouds, I will be like the Most High.'

"Yet you shall be brought down to Sheol, to the lowest depths of the Pit."

Isaiah 14:12-15

Note: *Dake's Reference Bible* indicates that "stars" in this scripture refer to angels.

Those fallen angels became demon spirits under Lucifer's control and direction. (Ephesians 6:12.) It is important to remember that two-thirds of the angels remained submitted and committed to God in Heaven, and they continue worshipping God and being God's agents to help people here on earth. They travel from Heaven back and forth ministering to those who are heirs of salvation. (See Hebrews 1:7,14; Psalm 91:11; Genesis 28:12.)

Verse 11 in the *New King James Version* says, **"Your pomp is brought down to Sheol, and the sound of your stringed instruments; the maggot is spread under you, and worms cover you."**

The *King James Version* describes the stringed instruments as "viols." In the Hebrew, "viols" is *"nebel,"* meaning several strings, violins, harps, guitars, etc. (Also see Psalm 150, verse 4, of *Dake's Bible.)*

Pride had entered Lucifer's heart along with the desire for God's position, so he rebelled against God's authority.

Satan walked up and down Heaven slandering God to the angels in order to get a following. One-third of the angels sided with Lucifer and rebelled with him. They were immediately cast down from Heaven with Lucifer. (See Revelation 12:4.)

In Luke 10:18-20 Jesus made reference to Lucifer's fall when seventy of the disciples had returned from ministering, using Jesus' name. They were excited that even demons were subject to them using the name of Jesus. Jesus replied:

"I saw Satan fall like lightning from heaven.

"Behold, I give you the authority to trample on serpents and scorpions, and over all the power of the enemy, and nothing shall by any means hurt you.

"Nevertheless do not rejoice in this, that the spirits are subject to you, but rather rejoice because your names are written in heaven."

Luke 10:18-20

In this instance, Jesus was teaching the disciples about not getting into pride or feeling superior. Pride and rebellion were the two reasons Lucifer and one-third of the angels fell from Heaven. Pride and rebellion lead to a fall (Proverbs 16:18).

Humility and submission to authority are important to God. Unless we are submitted to God's authority (the authority of His Word, to His Holy Spirit, and to those He has positioned in leadership), we will have no spiritual authority. We will also be open target to the enemy's deceptions. Remember, Adam and Eve had been under God's authority, but their disobedience in eating from the fruit of the tree God had forbidden, caused them to become deceived and open targets to the enemy.

AFTER SATAN WAS KICKED OUT OF HEAVEN . . .

The only way Lucifer (Satan) could retaliate against God once he was kicked out of Heaven, was to enter into the Garden of Eden and deceive what was most precious to God – mankind, Adam and Eve.

God had created mankind because He wanted a family. He created mankind different than all other species. It was mankind that God gave a heart to fellowship with Him. God loves people and desires relationship and fellowship with people, but He will not force people to love Him in return. He gave mankind the power of choice – a free will. God did this because He wanted mankind to love Him because they choose to love Him. The God-kind of love is not love without a choice. Without choosing to love, a person is just saying words that are empty. Love is a choice and an action we show.

Remember, God chose to first love us (1 John 4:19). Jesus chose to love us and die on the cross for us before we had responded to love Him in return. The God-kind of love that is the greatest love in the world chooses to do what will benefit others before itself. It is unselfish and giving. In fact, the love of God will give first before there is any response in return.

Satan has always had a counterfeit façade for everything God is, but his way of love always ends up empty with heartache and is even destructive. He was the reason Adam and Eve were driven from the Garden of Eden. He took what God had intended for good and turned it for bad. The good news is that what the devil intended for bad in a person's life can be turned for good when a person turns and chooses to love and obey God.

Chapter 2

An Explanation of Mankind as a Three-Part Being

God created mankind as a spirit, soul, and body. We are three-part beings. We are a spirit, we have a soul, and we live in a body. Both the spirit and the soul of a person are unseen to the natural eye. People only see the physical body.

1. The Spirit – the Heart of Man

God breathed into Adam His Spirit in Genesis 2:7. This is the part of man that longs to worship something because God put that part inside of mankind from the beginning. If someone doesn't worship God, then they find other idols to fill that part of them.

An idol is what you get your fulfillment and joy from. It is what you get your security in and your identity from. An idol doesn't have to be a wooden object. It can be a job, a title, another person, money, a place, a group of people you feel give you self-worth, a talent or ability that you might have, or any other thing other than God Himself. Your spirit is the part of you that can be born again when you receive Jesus' Spirit. He comes to live in your spiritual heart.

> **"And I will give you a new heart, and I will put a new spirit in you. I will take out your stony, stubborn heart and give you a tender, responsive heart.**
>
> **"And I will put my Spirit in you so that you will follow my decrees and be careful to obey my regulations."**
>
> **Ezekiel 36:26-27 NLT**

The New Testament calls your spirit "the inner man" (Ephesians 3:16); or "the new man" (2 Corinthians 5:17); or "the hidden man of the heart" (1 Peter 3:3). The New Testament helps us to see the three parts of mankind.

Paul the apostle wrote in 1 Thessalonians 5:23: **"Now may the God of peace Himself sanctify you completely; and may your whole <u>spirit</u>, <u>soul</u>, and <u>body</u> be preserved blameless at the coming of our Lord Jesus Christ."**

Notice, Paul makes a difference between the soul and spirit. I had always thought the soul and spirit were the same thing, but as I studied God's Word, I realized there is a difference, and it is important to realize the difference.

The spirit of a person can be born again and connected with God in relationship. However, if the person doesn't renew his or her mind to God's Word, that person will stay in wrong thinking and will be pulled into a wrong lifestyle.

THE IMPORTANCE OF PUTTING GOD'S WORD IN YOUR LIFE

I remember after I had surrendered my heart to the Lord, I had friends who had also surrendered to the Lord. I had heard God's voice within my spirit say to read my Bible and pray daily, so I did. However, I watched some of my friends get distracted away from their commitment to God. In talking to them, I realized they had not been putting God's Word in their lives. They were satisfied just attending church once a week, but feeding on things of the world around them and trying to get their source of fulfillment from those things. I find that reading the Word of God is different than reading other books. There is something supernatural about the Word of God.

Hebrews 4:12 NIV says, **"For the word of God is alive and active. Sharper than any double-edged sword, it penetrates even to dividing <u>soul</u> and <u>spirit</u>, joints and marrow; it judges the thoughts and attitudes of the heart."**

God's Word is alive. It's not just words on a page. God's Word reads you while you read it. It points out where you may be wrong or where you need to change. It corrects you, and yet it inspires you to grow in your relationship with God and with people.

Hebrews 4:12 affirms 1 Thessalonians 5:23 that there is a difference between the soul and spirit. Once we have received God's Spirit into our hearts and we begin to read God's Word, it separates what is of your soul and what is of your spirit. It lets us see what is of the soulish realm in our lives and what is of God's Spirit speaking to us.

2. The Soul

The soul is your emotions, your mind's reasoning, your will, and the seat of your passions. There are times when a Christian might say, "I felt led" to do something or not to do something. The person needs to ask himself or herself, "Is that feeling from my emotions, my own mind's reasoning, my own will, desire, and passions; or is it from my spirit?"

The characteristics of the spirit's leading will always be in line with God's written Word. The characteristics of our soul leading us will not be in line with God's Word. It will be self-focused. It will override consideration of others in its choices. It mainly does what benefits itself.

Notice, when Satan tempted Eve, he appealed to her mind (her reasoning), to her curiosity and human desire.

He made her question and then dismiss God's Word. He convinced her that she had been missing out and how she could have so much more. He made her think there would be no consequences to her choices; and when she didn't see anything at first, she thought she was doing good. She gave the fruit to Adam and their eyes were opened and realized they were naked and were driven from the Garden.

Paul, the apostle, told us to be renewed in the attitude of our minds (Ephesians 4:23). He wrote in Colossians 3:10 AMP, **"And have put on the new [spiritual] self who is being continually renewed in true knowledge in the image of Him who created the new self."** We do this by reading and meditating God's Word. It changes our thinking patterns to think differently than our fleshly nature thinks. We begin to see the importance of having boundaries in our lives.

3.   The Body

Our physical body is a shell that our spirit and soul live in. Medical science can cut open a person's physical body, but they cannot see into the spirit or soul of that person. The spirit and soul are invisible, but they have evident characteristics expressed through our body. The body acts out whatever the soul or spirit leads it to do.

The apostle Paul wrote how that he knew of the struggle between his soulish realm and his spirit. In Romans 7:14-25 AMP Paul wrote:

We know that the Law is spiritual, but I am a creature of the flesh [worldly, self-reliant — carnal and unspiritual], sold into slavery to sin [and serving under its control].

For I do not understand my own actions [I am baffled and bewildered by them]. I do not practice what I want to do, but I am doing the very thing I hate [and yielding to my human nature, my worldliness – my sinful capacity].

Now if I habitually do what I do not want to do, [that means] I agree with the Law, confessing that it is good (morally excellent).

So now [if that is the case, then] it is no longer I who do it [the disobedient thing which I despise], but the sin [nature] which lives in me.

For I know that nothing good lives in me, that is, in my flesh [my human nature, my world-liness – my sinful capacity]. For the willingness [to do good is present in me, but the doing of good is not.

For the good that I want to do, I do not do, but I practice the very evil that I do not want.

But if I am doing the very thing I do not want to do, I am no longer the one doing it [that is, it is not me that acts], but the sin [nature] which lives in me.

So I find it to be the law [of my inner self], that evil is present in me, the one who wants to do good.

For I joyfully delight in the law of God in my inner self [with my new nature],

But I see a different law and rule of action in the members of my body [in its appetites and desires], waging war against the law of my mind and subduing me and making me a prisoner of the law of sin which is within my members.

Wretched and miserable man that I am! Who will [rescue me and] set me free from this body of death [this corrupt, mortal existence]?

Thanks be to God [for my deliverance] through Jesus Christ our Lord! So then, on the one hand I myself with my mind serve the law of God, but on the other, with my flesh [my human nature, my worldliness, my sinful capacity – I serve] the law of sin.

Paul answers his thoughts about his struggle saying that Jesus Christ is our deliverance. Then, in Romans 8:5-6 AMP he states:

For those who are living according to the flesh set their minds on the things of the flesh [which gratify the body], but those who are

**living according to the Spirit [set their minds on]
the things of the Spirit [His will and purpose].**

**Now the mind of the flesh is death . . . but the
mind of the Spirit is life and peace [the spiritual
well-being that comes from walking with God . . . .]**

The mind is in the soulish realm. Our battle is in our
thought life. The good news is that we can take control of
our thoughts, and we can change our thinking by renewing
our minds to what God's Word says. We can set our minds
on the scripture and have the mind of the Spirit. Our bodies
will then follow our thought life in the right direction.

Not only is the physical body controlled by the soul
and spirit of a person, but also the physical body is affected
either positively or negatively by what is happening in the
soul and spirit. Most of the time a person's emotions, their
reasoning whether right or wrong, and their will determine the course and quality of their lives.

Paul realized the mind of a person has to be brought
into subjection to God's way of thinking. A person has to
renew his/her mind to God's Word by daily time in God's
Word and meditating the Scriptures.

God desires for the spirit of man to be submitted to
Him so He can work His will and His good pleasure in our
lives. He has a good plan for our lives, but we have to be
willing to hear and obey His voice. His voice on the inside
of our hearts will always be in line with His written Word.

Paul emphasizes in his letters to the churches that we must renew our minds to God's Word so that it supernaturally can change the course of our lives. It has been said, "As the mind goes, so the body follows." This is very true. We have to renew and protect our minds by guarding what we look at and what we listen to. Our eyes and ears are the gates or doors to our soul and spirit. Proverbs 4:23 in the *New Living Translation* tells us that we have to guard our hearts because the heart determines the course of our life.

We worship God with our spirit, soul, and body. The Psalmist said, **"Bless the Lord, O my soul; and all that is within me, bless His holy name!"** (Psalm 103:1). We tell our souls to bless the Lord, and we tell ourselves to bless Him with our whole being.

Jesus also affirmed this when He said the greatest commandment is to love God with all our heart, all our soul, all our mind, and all our strength. (See Mark 12:30.)

Chapter 3

LOVING GOD – THE MOST IMPORTANT COMMANDMENT

When asked, "Which commandment is the most important?" Jesus said:

"The first of all the commandments is: 'Hear, O Israel, the Lord our God, the Lord is one.

"'And you shall love the Lord your God with all your heart, with all your soul, with all your mind, and with all your strength.' This is the first commandment.

"And the second, like it, is this: 'You shall love your neighbor as yourself.' There is no other commandment greater than these."

Mark 12:29-31

Jesus said that love is the greatest of all commandments. First, we are to love God, and secondly, we are to love others as we love ourselves. When we love God, we will want to do what pleases Him. Jesus was saying that when we keep these two commandments of love, we will keep all the other commandments in the right perspective.

When God gave His commandments to His people, Israel, it was to bless and protect them and to set them apart from those who worshipped other gods. The Ten Commandments were given to show them how to honor God and honor the lives of others among them. The commandments weren't given to become a legalistic ritual. They were to give them guidelines for living. However, many of the religious leaders made them legalistic. God wanted relationship with His people based upon love.

When we keep these commandments, we will desire to keep the Ten Commandments, not from the attitude of a legalistic law, but from the attitude of wanting to show our love to God and others. (Also see Romans 13:8-10.)

When we worship God from sincere, passionate hearts, we are loving Him. Notice that Jesus emphasizes loving God with all our heart, all our soul, all our mind, and all our strength. Worship is one of the ways we express our love for God. He put the little word "all" in front of each of these parts because He wanted us to understand that people have the ability to love God halfheartedly. A person can sing and speak worship to God without putting any thought into it and doing it by rote. A person can worship God without expressing any emotion with their worship and just do lip service to God.

In Matthew 15:8 NLT Jesus said, **"These people honor me with their lips, but their hearts are far from me."** The sad thing is that this happens in many churches weekly if there are church members who have either never surrendered to the Lord or they have lost their first love for the Lord. In Revelation 2:4-5, John, the author of the book of Revelation, tells the church at Ephesus that they had lost their first love and needed to repent and remember how they had worshipped God with passionate hearts when they first got saved. Love flows out of a grateful heart. When we keep a grateful attitude, we will always love God with a sincere devotion.

LOVE ALWAYS HAS EXPRESSION

Jesus explains that we are to express our love to God from our heart, our soul, our mind, and physical strength. Some people say, "Well, I have a praise in my heart, but it's not my personality to be expressive." If that is the case, Matthew 12:34 says, **"Out of the abundance of the heart the mouth speaks."** In other words, you are going to talk about what is on your heart. You are going to want to sing about what is on your heart.

It is needful to evaluate why your personality at other times expresses its emotions, its words, and physical expressions about other things. Understand that whatever you are passionate about, you will talk about. Here is a natural illustration. I remember when I was dating my husband, I wanted to talk about him and talk to him. I wanted to be with him as much as possible. Remember, your soul is where your passion, your will, your thoughts, and your emotions reside. Your will can be very strong once you have set your mind to do something.

We can will to express our love to God, or we can will to not express our love to God. God gave us a free will to choose to love and obey Him, or choose not to. He doesn't force us to love Him. Love is not love apart from choice. Sometimes people don't want others to think they are extreme Christians. Why not? Jesus has had extreme love for you and me.

Stop and think. Jesus went to the cross by choice because He loved us, not because it felt good or because He had romantic feelings of love for us. He felt pain and He suffered, but He did it anyway because He chose to love us beyond His natural feelings.

Love is a choice, not a feeling. Sometimes feelings will be there, but sometimes they aren't there. We choose to love and we choose to worship when we don't feel like it. God has promised to meet us in that place of sacrificial praise and worship.

When we worship beyond our feelings, our feelings change. I can remember times when I have felt tired, anxious about our circumstances, and somewhat depressed. I have heard in my spirit to start praising God, dancing, and lifting my hands while singing. As I acted on that prompting within me and as I rejoiced while singing and dancing, my spirit lifted. I began to feel victory. Even though our circumstances did not change immediately, my attitude changed. I stirred up my faith within me as I worshipped. The circumstances eventually changed, and we made it through that time. Praise God!

We have gone through many times like this through the years, and through praise and worship we have seen God work supernaturally.

Chapter 4

WHEN PRAISE IS A SACRIFICE

Through Him, then, let us continually offer to God the sacrifice of praise, which is the fruit of our lips, giving thanks to His name.

Hebrews 13:15 MEV

Sometimes you praise God when you don't feel like it and you feel depressed or fearful. This is when it is a sacrifice.

A sacrifice costs something. It costs you moving beyond your feelings. It costs you letting go of self-aware-ness, pride, or fear of what other people may think. It costs you energy and effort to express your faith in God and your love to God no matter what circumstances look like. This is why the Psalmist wrote over and over:

I will bless the Lord <u>at all times</u>; His praise shall continually be in my mouth.

Psalm 34:1

Thus I will bless You while I live; I will lift up my hands in Your name.

Psalm 63:4

I will exalt you, my God and King, and praise your name forever and ever.

I will praise you every day; yea, I will praise you forever.

Psalm 145:1-2 NLT

The Psalmist understood the power of <u>his will</u>, and he spoke to himself saying, "<u>I will</u> bless the Lord."

I remember the first year we started our church. We were barely making it financially. It was a difficult time. Through the financial counsel of others, we had to let go of almost half of our staff. Some people were critical of us during that time.

We had sold our only car to pay a ministry bill. The day after that, Billy Joe's brother who was in the military called and asked us to keep and drive his car for the next year and a half. Praise God!

A few months before this when our youngest daughter was six months old, she almost died. She had been diagnosed with one of three diseases: leukemia, a rare type of pneumonia, or spinal meningitis. We had prayed and stood for her healing without telling a lot of people because we wanted only those who would agree with our faith and not speak negatively about her. She was miraculously healed, and the doctors said maybe they had misdiagnosed her. We knew God had healed her.

Also, during those months, one night our house was broken into and we saw the thief running and jumping over our back fence. We didn't have much so he didn't get much.

Then, after my husband went to work one morning, I received a threatening phone call that someone had kidnapped him and had a knife he was holding to his throat. He told me if I didn't cooperate with him, he would kill him. Out of my spirit came scriptures I had memorized of Psalm 91 and 1 Corinthians 3:17. The person hung up, saying that I had made my decision. Immediately, I called the operator, the police, and his workplace. Praise God! He was safe at work. It had been a prank call.

During this testing time, I remember one day I was feeling battle weary and in my time with God, I heard Him say, "Get up and sing, dance, and rejoice in the Lord." I did not want to. I told the Lord that the scripture said I could cry unto the Lord and He would hear me out of His holy hill (Psalm 3:4). Then I heard His voice again in my spirit say, "Rejoice in the Lord, sing, and dance."

I got up and began to do that at first crying as I did. However, the crying stopped as I chose to rejoice beyond my feelings. God told me to cast my cares upon Him, because He cared about me. I told Him I knew that scripture from 1 Peter 5:7. He then said to me, "Yes, but after you cast the care in the morning, you take it back when you lie down in bed at night. You need to cut the line." So I saw myself in my mind cutting the line on all of the various circumstances. Then, I chose to praise God beyond my feelings, and God worked in an amazing way.

Everything did not change immediately, but over the next year and a half, things did change and we came through that hard time.

A sacrifice of praise is praising God beyond how you feel. It is choosing to set your will to worship God and believe in His supernatural power. A sacrifice of praise is an act of faith beyond your feelings. Slowly things turned, and I grew a little more in my spiritual walk during that time.

Chapter 5

Worship Is About Relationship and Fellowship

David, the Psalmist, wrote:

My Lord, there is no God like you. No one can do what you have done.

My Lord, you made everyone. I wish they all would come worship you and honor your name.

You are great and do amazing things. You and you alone are God.

Lord, teach me your ways, and I will live and obey your truths. <u>Help me make worshiping your name the most important thing in my life</u>.

My Lord God, I praise you with all my heart. I will honor your name forever!

You have such great love for me. You save me from the place of death.

Psalm 86:8-13 ERV

This scripture lets us see that praise and worship is important in our relationship with God. God created mankind because He wanted a family to fellowship with. We fellowship with God in praise and worship. We speak or sing to Him, and He speaks to us as well. We were created to worship. We weren't created out of other species such as animals. When God created the heavens and the earth, He created mankind different than all other species of being (Genesis 1:24-31, 1 Corinthians 15:39).

Adam and Eve walked and talked with God in the beginning (Genesis 2:7,15-18; 3:8-21). Satan was as a serpent in the Garden. He also talked to them and he deceived them to eat the fruit of the one tree they were told not to eat from. The serpent was more subtle than any other beast. ("Subtle" means inconspicuous but with grave danger.) Always remember that Satan is subtle. He studies people to come at their thoughts with questioning, doubts about God, and deceptive offers, ultimately bringing heartache, pain, and regret. Adam and Eve ate the forbidden fruit. Immediately they lost fellowship with God because of sin.

However, God provided a way for them to come to Him by the blood of animals. He covered them with animal skins. The blood was to atone or cover their sin so sin could not stop mankind forever from having a relationship with Him. As time progressed and people multiplied in the earth, sin drew many away from God, their Creator. (See Genesis 6:9-14,17-19,22; 8:20-22; 9:1-4,12-13.)

God had a plan from the beginning that He would ultimately send His only Son into the world to regain what Adam and Eve had lost. (Genesis 3:14-15; Isaiah 7:14; Matthew 1:20-23; John 1:1-4,14; Colossians 1:12-17.)

Someone might ask the question, "Why did God put the tree of the knowledge of good and evil in the Garden?" Because God had given them free will to choose. He wanted them to choose to love and obey Him, but He would not force them to do this. Again, let me emphasize, love is not true love except by choice. God's love chooses to love in spite of circumstances. God's love chooses to love unconditionally. Our free will is very strong. God gave us free will to choose a relationship with Him. That relationship is based upon faith in His Word.

Relationship with God is about believing that He created us and has a plan for our lives and that He loves us. Psalm 139:13-18 and Jeremiah 1:5 describe how God formed us and covered us in our mother's womb. God has a good plan for our lives (Jeremiah 29:11; Ephesians 2:10). However, Satan has a different plan for our lives if we listen to him (John 10:10, 4-6).

Because we have a free will, we can choose to love and obey God and experience His plan, or we can choose not to and experience Satan's plan. Relationship is about choice. When we choose to walk with God, He will talk to us, teach us, and help us while we are living here on earth.

Relationship with God is based on faith that we believe He is and that He is a rewarder of those who diligently seek Him (Hebrews 11:6). We believe His Word that He is present by His Holy Spirit and that He will work supernaturally in our lives as we believe.

Faith believes when it cannot see with the natural eyes. However, faith in God is not mysterious or without substance. (Hebrews 11:10). God has stated that our faith is based upon His Word. God's written Word is the highest truth. When we hear that Word spoken, faith can come inside of our hearts (Romans 10:17). When we read and meditate that Word, faith will rise from within us to believe. We approach God with faith knowing He has said to draw to Him and He will draw to us. **"Draw near to God and He will draw near to you . . ."** (James 4:8).

I remember after I received the Lord and I had been seeking Him daily, I read that scripture and thought, "How do I draw near to God if He is already in my heart?" I heard that still small voice say within my heart, "Sharon, it's about focusing your mind upon Him and not on other things that are vying for your attention."

Any time we choose to draw to the Lord, rest assured, the enemy seeks to distract us with other needs for our attention. It takes an effort to make time to draw to the Lord, but He says when we do, He draws to us in all that He is.

Chapter 6

Praise and Worship Defined

Psalm 117:1-2 ERV tells us:

Praise the Lord all you nations. Praise him all you people. (Why?)

He loves us very much! The Lord will be faithful to us forever. Praise the Lord!

"Praise" means to commend, to applaud, to express admiration for, to celebrate, to speak or sing words of admiration or thanksgiving, to glorify, to magnify.[1]

We can praise God directly with our lives, or we can praise God indirectly by telling others about His greatness.

---

[1]   *Merriam-Webster's Dictionary; Baker's Evangelical Dictionary of Biblical Theology, and Bible Study Tools online.*

When we magnify the Lord, it is like taking a magnifying glass and making Him bigger in our minds than the circumstances around us. He is great and He can do great miracles when we believe and magnify Him.

"Worship"means to reverence and it means adoration, devotion, to express love for God and thanksgiving to Him, to honor the Lord. *Webster's 1828 Dictionary* says it best: "Worship is to honor with extravagant love and extreme devotion." God loves us so it blesses Him when we return love to Him.

True worship involves surrender and submission to the Lord. It is living our lives devoted to Him. Worship is not just a song we sing; it is a lifestyle we live. We live to bring Him honor. It is having a consciousness of His presence continually. It is walking in fellowship with Him and being sensitive to His voice.

"In worship we allow Him to speak to us. It is about an intimate relationship with God," worship leader and Psalmist Dennis Jernigan said. "Intimacy" can be defined as "in-to-me-see." It is saying, "Lord, You can look within my heart and adjust my life where it may need to be adjusted."

Worship is learning to live with an awareness of Him. It is listening to Him, obeying what He says, and living our lives to honor Him. Since worship is about honoring God, even how we treat other people reflects whether or not we are honoring God or honoring ourselves. The term "worship" is listed in the Bible 108 times, and mostly it is not used in the context of music, yet when we talk about worship, most people think about it as singing.

WORSHIP THROUGH OBEDIENCE TO GOD

Genesis 22:2 is an example of this. God spoke to Abraham, **"Take now your son, <u>your only son Isaac, whom you love</u>, and go to the land of Moriah, and offer him there as a burnt offering on one of the mountains of which I shall tell you."**

We know that Abraham had a son by Hagar by the flesh named Ishmael, but Isaac was the son of promise that Abraham and Sarah had by a supernatural miracle from God. I'm sure Abraham didn't tell Sarah what God had said. In fact, he told no one. He simply took wood and a knife to make an offering on one of the mountains.

Once they arrived, he told the two young men who had gone with them to stay at the foot of the mountain <u>until he and his son returned from worshipping God</u> (v. 5). In other words, Abraham believed God's promise from Genesis 17 that Isaac was the son that God had established His covenant with and to his seed after him. He believed that even if he slayed his son, God would raise him from the dead and he would live out God's Word.

When they went to the top of the mountain, they didn't have any instruments. They had no guitar or tambourine.

They just went up <u>to worship with their obedience</u>. Isaac asked his dad where the sacrifice was. His dad said, **"God will provide for Himself the lamb . . ."** (v. 8). He prepared the altar of wood, tied up Isaac, and laid him on the altar. As he lifted the knife, an angel spoke to stop and not to harm the child. God said, "Now I know you will not withhold what is most precious to you – your only son (v. 12). Now I will bless and multiply your seed, and your seed will possess the gate of their enemies. In your seed shall all the nations of the earth be blessed <u>because you have obeyed My voice</u>." (See vv. 17-18.)

God provided an animal caught in the bushes for Abraham to sacrifice to God, and Abraham named the place "Jehovah Jireh, the God who sees ahead and makes provision." <u>Abraham's worship was his submission and obedience to God</u>.

In 1 Samuel 15:22-23 MEV, God spoke through the prophet Samuel, **"Obedience is better than sacrifice, a listening ear than the fat of rams. For rebellion is as the sin of witchcraft, and stubbornness is as iniquity and idolatry. . . ."**

In this scripture, King Saul had not fully obeyed God's instructions. He wanted a little of God and a little of his own way. Samuel told him his rebellion was as the sin of witchcraft. (If you've wondered if witchcraft is okay, this scripture lets you know it is sin.) Witchcraft seeks to control. Rebellion is like witchcraft because it seeks to control and have its way. Stubbornness is as idolatry because a person exalts their opinion and their way above God's way.

God looks on the heart of a person, and He knows if they are willing and obedient, or if the person, like Saul, has learned how to perform and look good to people. God knows what is going on inside of a person. He can see if a person is making an effort to obey Him.

It is easy to sing worship in church, yet be living in rebellion to God's direction. This is why the Psalmist said:

> **"Search me, O God, and know my heart; try me, and know my anxieties;**
>
> **"And see if there is any wicked way in me, and lead me in the way everlasting."**
>
> **Psalm 139:23-24**

In worship we allow God to search our hearts; and if we need to admit we are wrong about something, we can in that moment be free to worship Him with sincerity.

Worship is about loving God and wanting to know Him more as we conform our lives to His Word. The more you hang around someone, you will know them and you will conform to their way of thinking. You will take on their view of life and their view of the world. Whatever we worship will be the center of our lives. Our lives will revolve around what or who we worship.

In Revelation 2:4 the Holy Spirit spoke to the church of Ephesus telling them that they had done good deeds and had not grown weary. They had been patient and had discerned those who were false prophets and seen them as liars. However, they had lost their first love with the Lord. If you need to return to your first love, the place of intimacy with the Lord, then do it.

Repent of going your own way, and draw to Him again. This is an act of faith. Don't let the devil convince you that you can't regain that intimacy. You can. God receives you just as you are.

Chapter 7

What Does It Mean to Worship in Spirit and in Truth?

In John 4:23-24 AMP Jesus said:

> But a time is coming and is already here when the true worshipers will worship the Father in spirit [from the heart, the inner self] and in truth; for the Father seeks such people to be His worshipers.
>
> God is spirit [the Source of life, yet invisible to mankind], and those who worship Him must worship in spirit and truth.

In this scripture passage, the disciples had left Jesus by a well outside of town and had gone into town to get food. While at the well, a Samaritan woman came to draw water.

It was not the normal time women came to draw water, and she thought she would be alone. Jesus asked her for a drink. She was surprised that He, being a Jew, spoke to her. Jewish tradition did not permit a Jew to speak with a Samaritan and definitely didn't permit a man to initiate conversation with a non-Jewish woman. She asked Him why He was speaking to her as a Samaritan woman. He replied that if she knew who was speaking to her she would ask Him for a drink.

She knew He didn't have anything to use to get water from the well so she asked Him how He would do this. He told her He would give her living water springing up into everlasting life. She asked Him to give her some of this water so she would not have to come to the well again. He then asked her to go get her husband. She replied that she had no husband.

Jesus knew by supernatural revelation that she had told the truth and that she had had five husbands. He told her that she was living with a man to whom she was not married. She was convicted about her sin and realized He was a prophet, so she changed the subject and began to ask Him where was the correct place of worship.

As she questioned Him about where they were to worship, Jesus responded that Samaritans really didn't understand what they worshipped, but that the Jews knew who they worshipped. However, He said that the day was coming that true worshippers of God would worship Him in spirit and in truth because God is a Spirit. God seeks those who worship Him in spirit and in truth. He let her know it was not about the place as much as it was about the heart of worship within each person.

There are certain insights in this scripture. First, Jesus loves all people, all genders and races, and He reaches out to people from every kind of background. Secondly, Jesus revealed the woman's heart. This woman had looked for her fulfillment, her security, and her identity in having a man in her life. No man could meet those needs in her heart. Only God can fulfill us and give us security and our identity. Thirdly, the woman didn't understand what worship really was about. It had been only a religious habit to her. It was not about a relationship with God to her.

True worship is a personal relationship with God through His Spirit. It is being in communion and conversation with Him. It is not a place we come and go. It is a place we live. You don't have to go around saying, "Praise the Lord, Praise the Lord" all the time. However, you become very aware that He is always with you, and there are moments in the day you acknowledge Him in praise and gratitude.

What is "worshipping God in spirit"? The two Greek words here are *"proskeneo,"* meaning to reverence and adore; to bow oneself in humility and submission; to kiss; an attitude of loving submission, like a dog licking the hand of its master. *"Proskeneo"* carries the connotation of someone who adores and loves the one they worship. The Greek word for "spirit" is *"pneuma,"* meaning breath of God. When God breathes His life into our hearts, we are awakened to His love and power. John 3:6 says, **"That which is born of the flesh is flesh, and that which is born of the Spirit is spirit."** Only those who have allowed Jesus to come into their hearts can truly worship in spirit. Being born again connects the spirit of a person to God's Spirit.

WHAT ABOUT "WORSHIPPING IN TRUTH"?

The Greek word for "truth" is *"alethia,"* signifying the reality lying at the base level. True worship is to come from the base level of our heart. It is not just mouthing words. It is meaning the words you speak or sing to God. It is loving God with your actions as well as your words. It is not just putting on a mask to look good in front of others. It is being truthful in your worship and having a sincere heartfelt love for God. It's not about a performance. It's about genuinely loving God from your heart, however He prompts you to express that love.

We also worship God with the truth of His Word. When we sing or speak His Word in worship to Him, we are agreeing with Him. Amos 3:3 says, **"Can two walk together, unless they are agreed?"** John 8:31-32 tells us that if we continue in His Word, we will know the truth and the truth will set us free. There is unity with God and freedom when we worship by singing or speaking His Word to Him.

Chapter 8

BIBLICAL WAYS OF WORSHIP

Some have said, "Just worship God in your own way!" I ask the question, "Where is that in the Bible?" Why not find out how God says we are to worship Him?

Hedonism says, "Whatever feels good, do it." Reverse Hedonism is, "Whatever you don't feel like doing, don't do it." Notice the term "feel." Our society today has been saying, "If you can't feel it, then it isn't real." Understand that your feelings are up and down. Your feelings change according to circumstances changing. People who live by their feelings are up and down and unstable.

You may not feel like taking a shower or brushing your teeth, but you know if you don't, others will not want to be around you. You may not feel like going to work each day, but if you want to get a paycheck, you do it anyway. You may not feel like getting up during the night to take care of a loved one, but you do it anyway because they depend upon you.

Everything about living the Christian life is about doing what we do by faith. Four times in scripture we are told, **"The just shall live by faith,"** not feelings. If Noah had lived by his feelings, he would have stopped building the ark and would have been drowned with his family and others. Everyone in the Bible realized they had to live by faith in what God had spoken when they could not see anything to support their belief at the moment except they knew they had heard from God.

In Joshua 6, we read the account of Joshua and the people of God going to possess the land that God had promised. The first city was Jericho. The wall around the city seemed impenetrable and impossible to break through. God said to Joshua to march around the city once a day for six days, making no noise. Then, on the seventh day, march around the city seven times. At the end of the seventh time around, blow the trumpets and shout with a great shout. They obeyed God and the walls fell flat, so the people of God went into the city and conquered it. Their shouting to God released God's supernatural power to work in their behalf. Notice, the impenetrable walls fell before them. It was their obedience, their faith, and their praise to God that brought those walls down.

God wants for walls to fall in relationships or in difficult situations we sometimes find ourselves in. Sometimes after we have obeyed God, we need to shout to God in those situations.

I wasn't raised in a church where there was shouting, except I remember one little older lady at times would say, "Hallelujah." The first time I shouted, I was concerned about other people hearing me, but they were shouting too. It's easier to shout when others are shouting too, but sometimes the Lord wants you to shout in your own prayer time with God as well. Later I read in scripture that there are times to shout to God "for" victory. Sometimes I have had to shout in order to see victory happen. This is a shout of faith that I believe God is working when I cannot yet see it.

I remember a few years back, a man in our choir was having marriage problems. His wife was saying she wanted a divorce. He told me that one day the Lord spoke to him in his prayer time to march around his house six nights in a row, each night quietly praying in the Spirit. The seventh night he went around his house quietly praying in the Spirit seven times, and at the end of the seventh time, he began praising God and shouting, "Hallelujah! Praise the Lord!" He said after that she began to slowly change and become open. She did not go through with the divorce.

This may sound foolish to some people. However, I believe God can give us strategies regarding what to do in each situation we face. This man heard God's strategy in prayer. He acted on it in faith, and he saw victory.

God wants us to see victory over the enemy in our spirits. This is why He has revealed various ways in His Word we can praise and worship Him.

We praise Him through:

Speaking our praise – Psalm 34:1; 35:28; Ephesians 5:19.

Singing – Psalm 28:7; 96:1-2; 149:1; Ephesians 5:19.

Clapping – Psalm 47:1.

Lifting our hands – Psalm 63:4; Lamentations 3:41; 1 Timothy 2:8.

Shouting – Psalm 47:1; 5:11; 35:27.

Dancing – Psalm 149:3; 150:4; 2 Samuel 6:14.

Making a joyful noise – Psalm 100:1; 66:1; 81:1.

Playing instruments – Psalm 149:3; 150:3-5; 33:2-3.

Kneeling – Psalm 95:6; Ephesians 3:14.

Standing – Psalm 134:1; Nehemiah 9:5.

Singing in the spirit and in the understanding – 1 Corinthians 14:15.

THERE ARE SEVEN HEBREW WORDS FOR "PRAISE"

1. *Yadah* – To extend or throw out the hand in worship (Psalm 63:4; 2 Chronicles 6:13).

2. *Todah* – To extend the hand in adoration and thanksgiving, thanking God for what He has done and what He is yet to do. Praising God in faith for victory before it is seen with the natural eye (Psalm 141:2; Nehemiah 8:6).

3. *Halal* – To be clear, to shine, to boast, to rave, to show, to celebrate, to appear clamorously foolish in praise. We get the word "Hallelujah" from this word (Psalm 149:5; 150:6).

4. *Shaback* – To shout, to address with a loud tone, to triumph and glory in the Lord (Psalm 32:11; 47:1).

5. *Barak* – To kneel as we bless the Lord in an act of humility and adoration; to bow down in a worshipful attitude (Psalm 95:6; 2 Chronicles 6:13).

6. *Zamar* – To touch the strings, used concordantly with instrumental worship (Psalm 150:3-5; 98:5-6).

7. *Tehillah* – To sing our *halal*, not ordinary singing, the highest praise from the flow of the Holy Spirit within a person (1 Corinthians 14:15).

I believe this is a place in praise and worship where we experience the Holy Spirit supernaturally moving among us. It is a time where believers wait upon the Lord to follow His lead. It can also be a time where believers sing prophetically. It can be a time where believers flow in worshipping in tongues. It is when Heaven and earth meet together. It is a time in worship where God can speak into hearts and a time where signs, wonders, and miracles can happen.

We can praise God anytime and anywhere – when we are at home alone, or when we are with others (Psalm 34:1; 119:62; 57:9; 150:1).

We have been commanded to praise God (Psalm 147:1), not because God is on an ego trip and needs it. God knows that as we praise Him, Heaven's help can come and the enemy is stopped. When we choose to praise and worship God, He is drawn to us with His help and all that He is (James 4:8).

Worship is being conscious of God's presence with us continually.

Chapter 9

What Is Worshipping God in the Beauty of Holiness?

Worship the Lord in the beauty of holiness; tremble before Him, all the earth.

Psalm 96:9 MEV

But like the Holy One who called you, be holy yourselves in all your conduct [be set apart from the world by your godly character and moral courage];

Because it is written, "You shall be holy (set apart), for I am holy."

1 Peter 1:15-16 AMP

What is holiness? Holiness is not based upon man's legalistic ideas. However, holiness in the life of the believer is obeying God, His Holy Spirit, and His written Word. It is living a life that is submitted to His ways and His thoughts. It is living set apart, placing restraints upon yourself because you want to glorify God in every part of your life. It is living with a consciousness of God being with you and in you. It is being sensitive in what you do or speak, evaluating whether it glorifies God or not. It is living devoted to God.

"Holiness" in the Greek is *"hagiamos,"* the same root word for sanctification; to be set apart unto God; to be consecrated to God; to be totally devoted to God.

Israel was set apart for God (Exodus 19:3-6), and they were to be holy. They were to be different than the world around them. They were to be devoted to God. It did not mean they were perfect like God. It meant they were to make the effort to obey God and His commands.

First Peter 2:9 says that we who receive Jesus Christ as Lord and Savior become **"a chosen generation, a royal priesthood, a holy nation, His own special people, that [we] may proclaim the praises of Him who called [us] out of darkness into His marvelous light."**

As believers in Christ, we are set apart and called by God to show forth His praise. When you show something, people see it. God wants people to see our praise and to see us live our lives in praise and honor to God.

Second Corinthians 7:1 tells us to **"cleanse ourselves from all filthiness of the flesh and spirit, perfecting holiness in the fear of God."**

1) "Filthiness of the flesh" are actions of sin. For example, we are told in 1 Thessalonians 4:1-8 that God's will is for us as Christians to stay away from sexual sin. Paul wrote to keep control over your body, to live in holiness and in honor to God, not in lustful passion like people who do not know God and His ways.

We are not to commit any sexual sin, and if we refuse to obey these commands from God, we are not rejecting human teaching, but we are rejecting God Himself who gives His Holy Spirit to us to convict us and convince us of sin. Sexual sin would include fornication, adultery, incest, homosexuality, and pornography.

I might add, as those in leadership, we are called by God to examine ourselves (2 Corinthians 13:5). If you ask the Lord, He will help you, even in the clothes that you wear, not to be a stumbling block to others. Our lives are an open book to others who watch us. No one is perfect, but we should seek to honor the One who is – Jesus.

I realize some have shoved aside the convicting voice of the Holy Spirit, but this is a dangerous place to be. When a person is living in known sin, they have opened the door to the enemy and they have closed the door of God's protection. God gives us His grace to repent, but if a person doesn't repent and they continue to reject God's warnings, the person is headed for trouble.

2) "Filthiness of the spirit" refers to wrong thoughts, attitudes, and wrong motives. It involves holding on to offences, bitterness, resentment, jealousy, pride, selfishness, lust, strife, fear, and other wrong thought patterns.

Hebrews 12:14-15 MEV tells us to **"pursue peace with all men, and the holiness without which no one will see the Lord, watching diligently so that no one falls short of the grace of God, lest any root of bitterness spring up to cause trouble, and many become defiled by it."**

The Psalmist wrote, **"Put me on trial, Lord, and cross examine me. Test my motives and my heart"** (Psalm 26:2 NLT). Hebrews 4:12 says that when we read God's Word, it is able to judge the thoughts and intents or feelings of our hearts. God looks upon our hearts, our thoughts, and our motives. This is why when we worship, we allow His Holy Spirit to search us and remove any thoughts or wrong motives from us. It is why we allow the Holy Spirit to convict and convince us of sin so we can confess it to God and repent. God can then have freedom to move in our lives, through our lives, and all around our lives. This is taking a heart checkup so that nothing blocks God's power in our lives.

Worshipping God in the beauty of holiness is to be aware of His holy presence as you worship. In His holy presence, you are allowing Him to have His way in your life.

Jesus said, **"Beware of the leaven** (influence) **of the Pharisees and the leaven** (influence) **of Herod"** (Mark 8:15), the Pharisees representing a legalistic, strict, excessive conformity to the law with no love, mercy, or compassion for others. They kept the law, but it was not about love for God. It was to make them look superior to others. Herod represents the world and its worldly direction. Many have allowed the world to pull them away from living consecrated to God.

Holiness produces a sensitivity in a person's heart toward God's holiness. It gives us an awareness of how we are to relate to others as Jesus would. Realizing our bodies are now the temple (house) of the Holy Spirit, Jesus lives in us. How could we make Jesus commit sexual sin? How could we make Jesus hold on to offense and unforgiveness? How could we speak abusively to others? Holiness is asking ourselves what would Jesus do in that situation? Holiness is asking ourselves, "Does this honor Jesus?" Holiness is realizing Christ is in you and seeking to live like Him and for Him.

Chapter 10

HINDRANCES TO PRAISE AND WORSHIP

There are hindrances that cause people to not express their praise and worship to God. Many times people make excuses that they do not praise and worship because it is not their personality to be expressive with their emotions. However, they express their emotions at other times without realizing it. The following list includes some of those hindrances.

1. **Lack of knowledge** (Hosea 4:6).

I was raised in church all of my life. However, we did not have teaching about praise and worship, In fact, our bulletin each week was titled "The Worship Hour." It listed two hymns, the Lord's Prayer, the Apostles' Creed, and a responsive reading that we spoke together, another hymn, offering and an offering special from the choir, announcements, a sermon message, another hymn, and a closing prayer. My spirit knew there was something more that we were missing.

In the 1970's, after I had received the baptism of the Holy Spirit, I attended charismatic churches. However, I still sensed in my spirit that most people were not yet understanding worship. I knew in my spirit that people didn't know why we sang songs and didn't seem to think about the words of the songs. I had found one or two worship recordings from Maranatha Singers and Christ For the Nations Institute. I was led by the Holy Spirit to make a small recording of some worship choruses because I believed God was awakening His Church to worship.

In the 1980's people began writing books, teaching people about praise and worship. More ministries began recording worship choruses for the Body of Christ internationally. Today churches around the world have grown in understanding the importance of praise and worship. I believe that the Holy Spirit is preparing us for Heaven. However, there are still some who haven't come to an awakening about worship, and sometimes this is because of a lack of knowledge.

2. Pride and stubbornness.

Pride says it is not my personality to express myself in worship. Stubbornness says you cannot make me worship. Sometimes people think that the worship team, like cheer-leaders, are trying to make them worship. This is how the enemy seeks to convince some people so they won't try to understand worship. He doesn't want them to enter into this part of their relationship with God. The worship team is trying to set the example of worship for believers to follow and experience passion for God and the Holy Spirit's supernatural touch.

Some Christians are embarrassed to express their praise and worship in front of others. While they will clap, lift their hands, shout, jump up and down at a ballgame, they find it too hard to do the same thing in church to God. Worship is not about us. It's about God. We have to evaluate if the Lord is on the throne of our lives or self is on the throne of our lives.

Don't let pride rob you of your worship experience with God. Be open to the Holy Spirit to His fresh truth in your life.

3. Hedonism and reverse hedonism.

Hedonism says if it feels good, do it. Reverse Hedonism says if it doesn't feel good, don't do it. It's all about your feelings. They say, "Worship God in your own way so everyone feels comfortable." There is no scripture to back this attitude. Jesus didn't say, "Follow Me if you feel comfortable." Living by feelings creates a self-focused, independent, rebellious attitude toward God.

Some say, "I don't have to be expressive in my worship to God because God looks on the heart." Right! God does look on the heart, and He can see if a heart is rebellious to His ways and stubborn or if the heart is yielded to His ways. He can see if a heart is grateful or ungrateful, proud or humble. God wants our hearts.

4. Fear and peer pressure.

When someone is more interested in what other people think about them than what God thinks about them, they are in fear of man. Proverbs 29:25 says, **"The fear of man brings a snare. . . ."** Ask yourself, "Do I seek to please God or man?"

5. Apathy, lethargy, and passivity.

Apathy is a lack of emotion, a lack of interest, and it is being indifferent. It is an "I don't care" attitude. It is an attitude that says, "Don't make me feel uncomfortable." Lethargy is a disposition of no energy and no passion for God. Matthew 24:12 says that one of the signs of the last days will be that as iniquity abounds, the love of many will grow cold. He is speaking here about believers' love for God growing cold and indifferent.

Some Christians have a passivity toward God. They have lost their first love for Jesus. This is one reason they are no longer inclined to worship. They've lost their passion for Him. Passion is an intense, compelling emotion that has an overpowering effect upon others. When there is no passion, there is no zeal. "Zeal" is being intensely devoted to God. It is a willingness to sacrifice one's own desires or feelings for the sake of God's will. Passion comes from spending time with God in prayer and in reading His Word. Then we choose to praise Him in faith.

When people choose to praise and worship beyond their feelings, they grow spiritually, and they keep their love relationship with God.

6. Casualness and looseness toward God.

This refers to a lack of reverence for God and His presence. Some appear to not be able to stand in God's presence as He begins to move among people. They become fidgety. They might chew gum or start talking to the person next to them or leave to go to the bathroom because they are convicted by the presence of the Lord. There is a resistance to the conviction of the Holy Spirit. They are easily distracted.

Another aspect of this looseness toward God is their lack of moral reverence. They see nothing wrong with living in sin and being a leader in worship. Every leader, whether leading worship or preaching, is responsible to

God for how they live their life. One day we will give an account of our lives here on earth before God.

7. Spectator worship.

Some believe that if they watch others worship, that is their worship as well. Only you can worship God for you. Spectators are contented that they have experienced worship by simply going to a service and watching others worship. Instead of standing back, critiquing and judging those leading worship, why not choose to enter into the worship? Stop and ask yourself if God is pleased with your attitude about worship.

8. Critical, faultfinding attitudes.

Some people feel it is their responsibility to stand and judge the worship and the people leading. They find fault and criticize instead of entering into the worship experience.

9. Sentimentalism.

This person feels that they can only truly worship if their favorite songs are sung. They connect true worship with the songs that were sung when they had a spiritual experience with God.

I remember a lady one time told me she could only truly worship when the song "He Touched Me" was sung. That's because that was the song that was sung when she received a miracle from God. There are many more songs that God has given through the years. He encourages us to be willing to "Sing a New Song" to Him (Psalm 96:1).

10. Being too time-conscious.

Most often services must contain the following elements: worship, prayer, teaching of God's Word, offering, and an invitation. There are obviously times that a service will go longer than usual. A leader has to be sensitive in this area. I've been in worship times when the Holy Spirit was moving in the worship going longer than usual and people were ministered to. I've been in other worship times when the worship went over an hour because of people's tradition and people were tired by the time the message was to be preached and they began to leave. There is a need for sensitivity in leadership to understanding time and the direction of the Holy Spirit.

11. Tradition.

Some people don't want any changes in the worship of their churches. They want to sing the same older songs they have sung. They don't like to sing new songs. The Psalmist tells us to sing a new song to the Lord (Psalm 98:1; 149:1). It's good to have some songs everyone knows, but it's also good to include some new songs, since the Holy Spirit is moving fresh today. Churches have to not become stuck in their traditional ways to reach this generation.

Some Christians get stuck in tradition as their worship experience. I remember a lady told me that she liked our church, but that she had to go where there were stained-glass windows to feel like she had had a worship experience. How sad! God can move in any place when hearts are open.

We need to understand that with each generation, God gives new songs because He wants to reach more people.

Psalm 96:1,3-4 NIV says, **"Sing to the Lord a new song; sing to the Lord, all the earth . . . Declare his glory among the nations, his marvelous deeds among all people. For great is the Lord and most worthy of praise; he is to be feared above all gods."**

Just like God gave the children of Israel fresh manna from Heaven daily, God has fresh songs to relate to people. This does not mean the older songs are discarded. However, each generation is learning to hear God's voice and are seeking to reach more people to be saved. Instead of complaining that our favorite songs are not being sung, why not pray for this generation to hear and write God's Word in song to relate to this generation.

In his book, *Exploring Worship,* author Bob Sorge states that "the generational transition in worship has existed over the centuries. In 1723 some older clergymen wrote that the new songs were not as melodious or established in their style. They stated that there were so many new songs that it was impossible to learn them all. They said that preceding generations went to Heaven without these new songs and they were not needed. Some felt the new songs were too worldly. Some thought that the new songs were focused too much on the instruments playing. Others thought that the new songs encouraged young people to stay out late."[2] These were statements made about hymns that were being written during the 1700's.

God can use new and older songs. The important thing is that the leadership must be worshippers as well. Worship is a heart issue. God is drawn to hearts that seek to worship Him in unity and in the leading of the Holy Spirit. It takes willing, flexible servant hearts to usher God's presence into a place where lives can be changed.

We must not get stuck in tradition so we cannot be flexible to the Holy Spirit's leading. "Blessed are the flexible for they will not be bent out of shape."

12. Being performance focused.

Some Christians like to watch people perform. Instead of worshipping, they stand back to critique the worship band and singers. We have to remember that worship is about God, not us. One person said, "Well, I didn't get

---

[2]   Bob Sorge. *Exploring Worship,* Oasis House Publishers, Canandaigua, New York, 1987, 136-137.

anything out of that worship." My response to that is, "Did God get anything out of your worship in that setting?"

When the worship team begins to be more performance focused than worship focused, the worship may be outstanding, but be void of the Holy Spirit moving in people. If lives are not being ministered to by the anointing, there needs to be some soul-searching in the worship team. The worship team needs to keep a desire and willingness to let God teach them His ways.

Isaiah 10:27 tells us that it is the anointing that destroys yokes off of people's lives and lifts burdens, taking them away. More than anything, we need His anointing to be able to flow to people.

The Psalmist said to **"make His praise glorious"** (Psalm 66:2). It's good to practice instrumentally and vocally to do your best so the sound of worship is pleasant for people to enter in and experience the Lord's presence. But allow time in His presence for Him to teach you His ways. It is good to also have some worship with the worship team that is not a rehearsal, but a time to flow in the Holy Spirit as well.

When a team is learning a new song, it is good to rehearse it so you can focus on ministering the song to the congregation. The new song doesn't have to be exactly like the recording of the song. A worship band needs to be able to flow with that. The more a worship band practices together, the more they are able to be flexible and yielded to God together.

13. Hardness of heart and dullness toward God can hinder a person from worship.

God is drawn to the broken and contrite heart. In Psalm 34:18, the word "broken" in the Hebrew meaning is "humble." The word "contrite" in the Hebrew has the connotation of someone who has been bruised. The bruise causes a sensitivity after that. God is drawn to those who have a sensitivity to His Spirit moving and to the needs of others. Being "contrite" causes us to be sensitive to His voice and sensitive to the setting we are in.

14. Familiarity.

The danger in any relationship is familiarity. In our relationship to God, we have to guard against this in our worship experience that we don't think about the words we are singing because the song has become so familiar. This is why it is good to sing a variety of songs and not the same song every week.

15. Being "feeling" oriented.

We are called to worship even when our feelings do not feel like it. Worship needs to inspire people to victory. God wants us to worship Him to the place of victory that He has established for us through Christ. There are times our worship will require us to sing in faith, believing in the promise of victory that Jesus has given.

WORSHIP OPENS THE DOOR FOR THE HOLY SPIRIT TO MOVE

Congregational worship's main purpose is to create an atmosphere that the Holy Spirit can use to transform lives. This means leaders need to take time to meditate God's Word to know God's thoughts and ways. God will use both new and older songs that the congregation already knows. Sometimes if a song is familiar, people do not have to look at the words and their hearts are opened up for God to speak to them.

Songs that have repetitious lines and a melody that is easy to follow are easier to learn, and they stay with the people after the worship experience.

As we worship God in spirit, our worship opens the door to the Holy Spirit to supernaturally move among people. The supernatural gifts of the Holy Spirit are activated through worship. This is why Elijah called for an instrumentalist to play when King Ahab called him to prophesy what would happen as he and Jehoshaphat went out to battle. When the instrumentalist played, the hand of the Lord came upon Elijah, and he spoke what God was saying to the two kings (2 Kings 3:15-19).

Chapter 11

PSALMS, HYMNS, AND SPIRITUAL SONGS

Ephesians 5:19-21 and Colossians 3:16 tell us to sing psalms, hymns, and spiritual songs.

"Psalms" – Singing scriptures. Many worship songs have been written from the Old Testament books, such as Psalms, Isaiah, Exodus, 1 and 2 Chronicles, etc. Scripture songs were what the early Church sang, and they comprised these in a hymnal. People learned the scriptures by singing them.

"Hymns" – These are songs based upon the doctrine of the Scriptures. The Gospels of Matthew and Mark made reference to Jesus and the disciples singing a hymn (Matthew 26:30; Mark 14:26).

Over the centuries, hymns have been written that contained doctrinal belief. These were songs of human composition, composed by an individual under the creative anointing of the Holy Spirit. The lyrics or words are not copied directly from scriptures, but instead are formed into words by a person with poetic direction and set to a singable tune. Today's hymnals in many churches contain hymns written in the 1700's, 1800's, and early 1900's, but many songs and choruses written today qualify under the category of hymns.

"Spiritual Songs" – These are songs of the Spirit, spontaneous songs of the moment that arise from our spirits unto the Lord. It can also be a song that drops into a person's heart and mind as a word from the Lord for the moment.

The following are types of spiritual songs:

A. Singing a spontaneous praise, centered around one sustained chord.

B. Singing praise spontaneously to a set chord progression and tempo that all can join in singing, birthed out of thankfulness and praise.

C. Singing a prophetic word that flows with what God wants to be communicated at the time in a church setting (1 Corinthians 14:4,14-15). It can be a gift of prophecy or a gift of a tongue and gift of interpretation in the Spirit with a message to the people gathered.

D. Singing by the revelation of the Holy Spirit a complete song with verses and chorus that the congregation can sing as well.

The Holy Spirit desires to move and speak in worship, releasing His gifts among His people. People can recognize the difference in just singing Christian songs and singing with the anointing of the Holy Spirit. Anointed worship creates an atmosphere of freedom for God to move in lives supernaturally.

God can use every form of music for His glory when people have yielded themselves as vessels for God to use.

GOD USES PSALMS, HYMNS, AND SPIRITUAL SONGS

Some people have thought that the newer worship songs are not as spiritual as older ones. I find that people connect with whatever songs are being sung when they have very special spiritual experiences. Sometimes they think those songs are the only ones with which they can have a worship experience. However, as we said before, that is called sentimentalism.

God has always given new songs throughout the centuries and decades. With every move of God, new songs are given to believers for worship. Every setting is different, God will use new and old, but He wants to be the One who decides. If we can trust in the Lord and trust those who lead to hear from the Lord, we will not become frustrated.

Each generation and each ethnicity has their preferences musically. When people come together, they have to become willing to adjust and allow God's Spirit to work in their lives in the praise and worship. Sometimes we have to drop our preferences and receive from what God is using to communicate with at the moment.

In 1 Chronicles 16:4-6 and 1 Chronicles 25:1-7, we read how King David appointed certain Levites to praise and worship and record the songs they were receiving from the Lord. King David was a musician and Psalmist. He had received songs from the Lord while growing up as a shepherd in the fields watching after his sheep. Once he became King, he instituted praise and worship day and night in God's house. He set apart Asaph, Herman, and Jeduthun, along with their sons and daughters, to prophesy with singing and with harps, psalteries, cymbals, and horns.

They prophesied in song and music. Prophecy in scripture is to edify (build up), exhort, and comfort. It is to proclaim the Word of the Lord; to exhort and instruct with the Word of the Lord; to declare future events. It can also be when a person interprets, explains, or communicates sentiments or thoughts prompted by passion or feeling.[3]

---

[3]   Noah Webster. 1828 *American Dictionary of the English Language.*

In 2 Kings 3:15 Elisha called for a musician to come and play so he could hear from God His supernatural revelation and direction that was needed by the King.

THE ROLE OF ANOINTED MUSIC

Anointed music will drive away evil spirits and change the atmosphere.

In 1 Samuel 16:23, King Saul had not obeyed the Lord many times, and God removed the anointing as a leader from him. He could not hear God's voice anymore. An evil spirit came to torment him. His servants suggested getting an anointed musician to come and play, so they got David the young shepherd who was an anointed musician. As David played and sang, the evil spirits would leave Saul temporarily.

Music is a spiritual force, and when music is anointed it has spiritual power.

Isaiah 10:27 states that the anointing destroys the yoke of Satan's oppression and lifts the burden from off of a person. Anointed worship music breaks off the enemy's oppression. Flesh-driven music opens the door to wrong spirits that can create lust, depression, moodiness, pride, etc.

When we understand the power of anointed music and worship, we can move into the supernatural realms of the Holy Spirit. First Corinthians 14:1 tells us to desire the spiritual gifts and especially desire to prophesy.

The first person my late husband and I prayed for to be delivered from demon possession was a little older woman in a nursing home. She was tied to a wheelchair because she would attempt to grab people's hair or whatever she could get. She cursed continually with vulgar language. Her eyes were bloodshot because she could not sleep more than two hours at a time.

We prayed in the Spirit. We bound the demons in Jesus' name. She got louder as we got louder. Finally, my late husband told me to sing "Jesus Loves Me." As I did she began to groan and cry, saying, "Let me out; let me out; I'm tired."

My husband laid hands on her one more time, peacefully commanding the devil to leave her. Suddenly she dropped her head and fell asleep. The nurse rolled her out to another room and told us later that the woman slept the longest she had ever slept in three years. When she awoke she didn't remember anything about what had happened.

The Holy Spirit can give us direction as we are prayerfully sensitive to His voice. The Holy Spirit's directed song broke the power of the enemy off of her, and she received deliverance through the laying on of hands.

Chapter 12

UNDERSTANDING THE SPIRITUAL BATTLE AND MUSIC, PRAISE, AND WORSHIP

Matthew 4:1-11 gives the account of Jesus being led by the Spirit into the wilderness to fast and pray forty days. At the end of that time, Satan came to tempt Him when He was physically hungry.

Satan tempted Jesus with three temptations. One of the temptations was that Satan took Him to a high mountain where He could see the kingdoms of the world and the glory of them. Satan told Jesus that he would give Him all of it if He would just bow down and worship him. Immediately Jesus said, **"Away with you, Satan! For it** is written, 'You shall worship the Lord your God, and Him only you shall serve'" (v. 10). The devil left Him for a season of time.

Satan wants our worship. The term "worship" in this scripture means complete surrender and submission. Satan wants our surrender to him.

MY SURRENDER PERSONALLY CHALLENGED

I remember when I was younger I had an opportunity to go with a record label because of my singing. My late husband and I had only been married four years. We were traveling in ministry at the time preaching in churches. I had made two recordings on my own to sell as we traveled. The recording label was Christian and very appealing. However, it required that I travel on my own, promoting myself singing.

I already had established the fact that I was called with Billy Joe in ministry when we got married. I had had the call of God on my life as a teenager, and when I married we knew we were called together as a couple. This recording company treated us to a nice hotel and a meal to talk, but I knew immediately in my spirit that I wasn't to do it.

So many times I've watched Satan appeal to the young generation starting out, dangling the golden carrot of opportunity, fame, and fortune before their eyes, but there many times is a catch. I've seen gifted people lose their close walk with the Lord over fame and fortune. One compromise can lead to another.

Please understand, I realize that God leads people in different ways. Some have been led in concerts and traveling. I am just aware that there are some who were led away from God's plan subtly, not realizing it until they began to lose what was precious to them along the way.

I believe my foundation of surrender in the beginning of my walk with God and putting His Word in my life daily gave me some stability to rightly discern what I was being offered.

Years later I was offered another opportunity to be used singing and traveling with a well-known ministry. However, it would have required me to be away from my husband and our church in traveling monthly. I thanked them for the opportunity, but I knew where I was called to be.

I never regretted my decisions in either of these moments. I've gone through seasons in my life where I was home more raising children and being available to my husband in our church. I have also had seasons of pastoring not only by his side, but being lead pastor for a season before transitioning to my son. In every season, I have known that I have been in God's will and have had peace about it. The most important thing is knowing the leading of the Holy Spirit.

Today I'm in a season of teaching, leading worship in a weekly service, traveling in ministry, overseeing prayer ministry, and representing our church in affairs with praying for government and for Israel. If we can come to a place where we can say, "Lord, if You can use me better over here than over there, then I am willing." My identity is in the Lord, not in my title or position.

SUITING UP DAILY IN GOD'S ARMOR

Ephesians 6:10-18 tells us we are in a spiritual battle with demonic spirits opposing us in our calling with God here on earth. We are told that in order to be strong in the Lord and in the power of His might and overcome the enemy, we have to put on the whole armor of God. This includes:

1. Our loins girded with truth;
2. The breastplate of righteousness;
3. Our feet shod with the preparation of the Gospel of peace;
4. The helmet of salvation;
5. The shield of faith;
6. The sword of the Spirit, which is the Word of God; and
7. Praying always with all kinds of prayer in the Spirit.

We need to know our position of authority in Christ according to scripture. (See Ephesians 1:16-23, 2:6; Matthew 28:18-20; Mark 16:17-18; Luke 10:19; 1 John 4:4.)

In Matthew 8, we read that the Roman centurion understood that Jesus had authority because he was submitted to a higher authority, God. We have authority as we are submitted to God's authority.

Second Corinthians 10:4-6 KJV states that we've been given weapons of warfare to fight the fight of faith:

(For the weapons of our warfare are not carnal, but mighty through God to the pulling down of strong holds;)

Casting down imaginations, and every high thing that exalts itself against the knowledge of God, bringing into captivity every thought to the obedience of Christ;

And having in a readiness to revenge all disobedience, when your obedience is fulfilled.

In Rick Renner's book, *Sparkling Gems,* the word for "warfare" in the Greek is *stratos.*[4] *Stratos* is where we get the word "strategy." The word "carnal" means anything of the flesh or anything of the natural realm. In prayer, God can give the believer supernatural strategy and insight.

The Holy Spirit gives us strategies in prayer from God to pull down strongholds of the enemy. Ephesians 6:11 tells us the enemy has schemes or strategies and deceits,

---

4   Rick Renner. *Sparkling Gems,* Teach All Nations Publishing, 2003, 106.

but God gives us strategies by praying in the Spirit and meditating God's Word to overcome him that are mighty through God. Particularly, we have to pull down strongholds in the mind or in our thoughts and cast them down in Jesus' name. When we praise and worship God, we pull down strongholds of thoughts that attempt to challenge our faith in God.

Knowing that praising God stops the enemy and brings us strength (Psalm 8:2), we praise and worship God in faith, believing God is faithful to His Word. Praise brings strength from God and silences the enemy's negative thoughts.

Abraham, being fully persuaded and strong in faith, gave glory to God that what He had promised He was able also to perform (Romans 4:16-21). Abraham understood his worship to God was vital to believing for a miracle in having a son with Sarah when they were past the age of childbearing. It looked impossible for them to have a child in their old age, but God willed for them to have Isaac as a miracle testimony that God could do anything. Praise and worship gives us strength in hard times, but also dampens and quiets the enemy's thoughts.

> **Out of the mouth of babes and nursing infants You have ordained strength, because of Your enemies, that You may silence the enemy and the avenger.**
>
> **Psalm 8:2**

Jesus quoted this verse in Matthew 21:12-16. In this account, Jesus rebuked those who were selling animal offerings and taking advantage of the people. He went inside the temple and began healing the blind and the lame. When the chief priests saw this and heard the children shout, **"Hosanna to the Son of David!"** (v. 15), they rebuked Jesus for allowing the children to say this. Jesus responded with the scripture of Psalm 8:2. However, He quoted it, saying, **"Out of the mouth of babes and nursing infants You have perfected praise"** (v. 16).

In this statement, Jesus was inferring that not only when natural children but also when spiritual babes in Christ (new believers) praise God, He can fulfill the rest of Psalm 8:2. When we praise God, He can perfect (mature) our praise and use it to bring His strength into our lives. Our praise silences the enemy in our minds and stops him from defeating us.

Scripture tells us over and over, "Praise the Lord!" Praise is a command from God, because He knows what praise can do for us.

PERSONAL TRIUMPH THROUGH PRAISE AND WORSHIP

I remember years ago we were walking through a difficult trial that lasted about two years. A number of people had left our church and gone to a different church. Each sent a letter that looked similar as if they had gotten together, written the letter, and then sent it separately. Of course, this was not the case. The enemy brought lying imaginations to my mind. Also, I was made aware of some deception going on that I could not speak about. I remember crying to the Lord for the friends I had known through this situation.

One night I spoke to my husband as I cried and said, "This is not right." My husband asked me, "What are you teaching right now in Victory Bible College?" I answered, "Praise and Worship." Then he said, "Okay, let's praise and worship God." I told him, "I know that, but scripture tells me I can also cry unto the Lord, and He will hear me out of His holy hill" (Psalm 3:4).

My husband said, "Okay, you've cried already. Now let's praise and worship." Then he began to lift his hands and praise God and dance around the room. At first it irritated me that he did not support me crying. Then I realized how right he was. I began to praise and worship with him.

Praise and worship got my mind off of the problems and got my mind on to God who was above it all. God worked in the situation, and we saw Him work in the lives of people.

Praise and worship can carry us through difficult situations as we turn to Him. Praise and worship can strengthen us and give us a resilience in our attitude to overcome.

Scripture gives us various weapons (strategies) to overcome the devil. These weapons include:

1.   The blood.

Revelation 12:11 says:

> **"And they overcame him by the blood of the Lamb and by the word of their testimony . . . . "**

Several years ago, I had officiated at the funeral of a young man from a low income apartment housing we had ministered in. He had just gotten his life right with the Lord, and a gang drove by, shot and killed him. His mother was a woman of prayer and had opened her home to young people to come if they needed prayer. She also spoke at the funeral challenging the young people there to commit their lives to the Lord. I gave an invitation and a few of them acknowledged they wanted to receive Jesus that day.

After that, I was worshipping the Lord in my home. I knew the scriptures about God's protection. I knew people needed to be encouraged in their faith at the time. God gave me a song about being "Under the Blood." Revelation 12:11 says we overcome the devil by the blood of the Lamb and the word of our testimony. It's important to remember that the blood of Jesus has power today as we sing about it and decree that we are under His blood as it covers our lives.

JESUS' BLOOD GIVES THE ENEMY NO ENTRY!

I was reminded of the people of Israel when they were in captivity in Egypt how God told Moses to sprinkle the blood of a spotless lamb over their doorposts one night. That same night the Destroyer spirit swept through the land, killing the firstborn in every home, except it passed over every Israeli home, and they were not harmed (Exodus 12).

When we declare the blood of Jesus is over our lives, we are speaking into the spiritual atmosphere that Satan cannot touch our lives. We are in blood covenant with God Almighty through Jesus Christ. Through our praise with scripture and our declaration of the blood of Jesus Christ in our lives, we are saying, "We give the devil no place" (Ephesians 4:27). We give him no entry point.

Praising God for the blood of Jesus gives strength to our lives. Praising God with His promises (scripture) is powerful as well, because God will agree with Himself – with what He has already spoken. Faith will rise in our hearts when we sing or speak His Word and promises.

Psalm 149:6-9 says that we are to let the high praises of God be in our mouth and a two-edged sword in our hand, which is the Word of God. Verse 8 says that praise binds kings and nobles. Daniel 10:11-14,20 MSG reveals to us that there are demonic angel princes (nobles) who reside over territories; and when we pray and praise God, it binds those spirits so God's angelic spirits can get through with answers to our prayers.

2. The Word of God.

Jesus gave us the example of using scripture to overcome the devil in Matthew 4:1-11. Jesus had just come off of a forty-day fast, and He was hungry. Satan came to tempt Him in His vulnerable time. Each time He was tempted, Jesus responded with scripture pertaining to the temptation by saying, **"It is written."** As He quoted scripture, Satan backed away. However, with one of the temptations, Satan quoted a scripture. Jesus was not taken off guard. He quoted scripture back at the devil, refusing his deceptive use of scripture.

Jesus could have used supernatural power to knock out the devil. Instead, He gave us an example to use the scripture to stop the devil's imaginations and temptations that he would try to bring against us.

God's Word is alive and is a powerful sword that is two-edged. One author, Rick Renner, said that one side of the sword is that God spoke it, and the other side of the sword is that we speak. When we speak it with faith believing in its power, the devil has to flee (Hebrews 4:12; Ephesians 6:17). When we sing the Word of God, faith rises in our hearts to believe for God's divine intervention in our lives.

3. **The name of Jesus.**

Proverbs 18:10 NIV says, **"The name of the Lord is a** [strong] **fortified tower; the righteous run to it and are safe."** Psalm 44:5 NCV says, **"With your help we pushed back our enemies. In your name we trampled those who came against us."**

One time, as I was ministering to a group of women about the power of the name of Jesus, I said, "If you are threatened or in a dangerous situation, call out that name." Years later, Vienna Schuering shared with me that her husband had become psychotic and she had been concerned for her life being threatened.

One day after that meeting her husband pinned her against the wall in her house with his hands squeezing around her neck and his face blurred with fury. She remembered, "Call out to Jesus." When she called out "Jesus," her husband released her neck and fell to his knees, begging her to let him go, screaming as she had her hand on his shoulder. "You're burning me. Stop touching me." Vienna said she was praying in tongues and continuing to say, "Jesus, save us."

The police came and arrested her husband who, by that time, was as docile as a lamb. There was a meeting with the Assistant District Attorney in Wichita, Kansas, and a hearing before the judge. The situation was resolved. She divorced him and later remarried.

She now oversees a women's ministry in her church to women who have had hardships and many have been abused. God not only delivered her life, but is using her life today because she believed and called on that name that is above every name.

4. **Prayer.**

Romans 8:26-27 says:

"Likewise the Spirit also helps in our weaknesses. For we do not know what we should pray for as we ought, but the Spirit Himself makes intercession for us with groanings which cannot be uttered.

"Now He who searches the hearts knows what the mind of the Spirit is, because He makes intercession for the saints according to the will of God."

"But he who prophesies speaks edification and exhortation and comfort to men" (1 Corinthians 14:3).

"What is the conclusion then? I will pray with the spirit, and I will also pray with the understanding. I will sing with the spirit, and I will also sing with the understanding" (1 Corinthians 14:15).

There is power in praying in tongues and in our understanding. When we don't know what to do or how to pray, we can pray in tongues and the Holy Spirit partners together with us praying God's will in situations. Our own understanding at times is limited, but the Holy Spirit is not limited. Praying in tongues allows our spirit to pray. Then the Holy Spirit will begin to reveal to your understanding what you are praying.

5. **Praise and worship.**

"Let God arise, let His enemies be scattered; let those also who hate Him flee before Him" (Psalm 68:1).

Praise can cause the enemy to defeat himself. In the story of 2 Chronicles 20:21-23, as Jehoshaphat and his army went out to battle while praising God, their enemies began to fight each other and defeat themselves.

6. **Faith.**

"Fight the good fight of faith, lay hold on eternal life, to which you were also called and have confessed the good confession in the presence of many witnesses" (1 Timothy 6:12).

"For whatever is born of God overcomes the world. And this is the victory that has overcome the world – our faith" (1 John 5:4).

In this spiritual battle, we are fighting our enemy with faith in God and faith in His written Word. There is a reason that our modern culture tells the young to question everything. Satan's deception is the same as it was in the Garden of Eden. If he can get you to question God's Word, he can deceive you to no longer believe and no longer have any faith to fight him.

Every person, not only in the Bible, but throughout Christian history, who has ever done anything for God, making an impact on this world, had to live by faith. Faith is our overcoming victory over the devil.

7. **Love.**

"For in Christ Jesus neither circumcision nor uncircumcision avails anything; but faith working through love" (Galatians 5:6).

Love is a powerful weapon. First John 4:18 tells us, **"There is no fear in love; but perfect love** (Greek *telios* meaning mature or complete love) **casts out fear. . . ."** God's love is perfect, and He lives inside of every believer. His love enables us to do whatever He says without fear.

I remember reading the story of David Wilkerson, as a young preacher becoming burdened in his heart about the gang members in New York City. He saw where a quadriplegic had been murdered by gang members there, and he left his home to go reach this gang. It made no sense to the natural mind, because he did not know these people. He had prayed for their salvation. In faith and obedience to God's calling, he went. His wife was very pregnant, but she agreed he should go.

Once there, he found where they hid as a gang. They threatened his life. On one occasion, Nicky Cruz, one of the gang, held a knife at him, saying, "If you say 'God loves you and I love you, Nicky,' one more time, I'm going to cut you into a million pieces."

David said, "Nicky, you can cut me into a million pieces, and every piece will still cry out, 'God loves you and I love you.'"

Later, Nicky got saved. Nicky told us that he tried to stab David, but there was an invisible shield that stopped him. That gave him nightmares and daily torment. That was the shield and the weapon of love in its present form.

When we understand not only God's love for us, but that His love through us has power, we will not be afraid to obey whatever God says.

> **"For love is as strong as death . . . Many waters cannot quench love, nor can the floods drown it. . . ."**
>
> **Song of Solomon 8:6-7**

> **"Love never fails. . . ."**
>
> **1 Corinthians 13:8**

Chapter 13

PRAISE CAN RELEASE HEAVEN'S INTERVENTION

Second Chronicles 20 contains the story of Jehoshaphat and the people of Israel when they were surrounded by enemies. It looked like there was no way out of the situation. It looked impossible. As they prayed and fasted, God spoke through one of the men prophetically:

> "**Do not be afraid or discouraged because of this vast army. For the battle is not yours, but God's . . .**
>
> **You will not have to fight this battle. Take up your positions; stand firm and see the deliverance the Lord will give you . . . Go out to face them tomorrow, and the Lord will be with you."**
>
> **2 Chronicles 20:15,17 NIV**

After Jehoshaphat and the people bowed and worshipped God, he arose and said, **"Believe in the Lord your God, and you shall be established; believe His prophets, and you shall prosper"** (v. 20). Then he sent singers out in front of the army singing, **"Praise the Lord, for His mercy endures forever"** (v. 21).

As they sang, the enemies began to fight and destroy each other. Israel watched this amazing sight. God had sent His angels to fight the battle just as it had been said, and they took the spoils that day. Notice, they had to believe the word of the prophet and act upon it. Jehoshaphat acted on the prophecy and by putting the praisers out in front, God sent angels to fight for them and cause the enemies to defeat themselves.

Psalm 22:3 tells us that God inhabits the praises of His people. All that He has and is comes to minister to us when we praise and worship Him. Praise and worship in the midst of trials and difficulties goes against our mind's reasoning. We have to press into praise and worship many times when our minds, emotions, and sometimes our bodies feel pain or when our minds struggle with fear. Choosing to praise and worship requires faith and trust in God that He is for you and He is with you.

When our daughter Sarah and son-in-law Caleb were moving overseas to live in Hong Kong and minister throughout Asia, while on the plane, their three-year-old son, Isaac, stopped breathing. Sarah called on the name of Jesus and prayed in tongues. Caleb began to do CPR on Isaac. They called for help. There just happened to be a pediatric nurse sitting close to them, a pediatric hematologist on board, and an ER person on board.

As they were able to get his breathing restored, Isaac had another episode before the plane landed. They took him to a hospital when they arrived. The tests they took did not reveal anything. They went to the place they were to stay, and Caleb traveled on to preach where they were scheduled while Sarah stayed with their two children.

The enemy tried to create fear and questioning in Sarah's mind. Suddenly she remembered a praise song and began to sing praise. As she sang, "No weapon formed against me shall remain. I will sing praise," God began to assure her in her heart that He was working in Isaac.

We were praying back here as well. God gave me a scripture from Isaiah 57:19: **"I create the fruit of the lips: peace, peace to him who is far off and to him who is near," says the Lord, "and I will heal him."**

I believe there's power in praise and worship and in getting revelation from God as we praise and worship, and He will work beyond what we could do.

In John 9 we read how that Jesus had healed a man blind from birth. When the Pharisees questioned the man about Jesus healing him, the man replied, **"Now we know that God does not hear sinners; but if anyone is a worshiper** of God and does His will, He hears him. Since the world began it has been unheard of that anyone opened the eyes of one who was born blind. If this Man were not from God, He could do nothing" (vv. 31-33).

Of course, the Pharisees did not like him saying this and they rebuked him. However, this common man saw that Jesus was a worshipper of God, He was obedient to God, and that Jesus had power to heal.

Psalm 62:11 says, **"God has spoken once, twice I have heard this: that power belongs to God."** Worship, faith, and obedience draw upon God's supernatural power in our midst.

Whenever I go to minister, I believe it is important to worship and then have believers pray for one another, expecting miracles to happen. So many miracles have happened over the years.

I remember one woman was healed of multiple sclerosis and walked out of her wheelchair. She is still healed today. I shared her testimony, and another woman who heard it and had been in a wheelchair over nine years, came and received prayer. She also was healed.

In another meeting, we worshipped and had people pray for one another. A woman who was born with osteoarthritis and had had it for sixty years was healed as she prayed for someone else. Worship can create an atmosphere for miracles to happen.

We are now on the threshold of a great awakening and move of God. Our world is so in need of God's Spirit transforming lives supernaturally. I believe God will fulfill His Word that in the last days, He will pour out His Spirit on all flesh; sons and daughters will prophesy, old men will dream dreams, young men will see visions as He pours His Spirit out on both men and women, young and old. (See Joel 2:28.) The beginning of this last day outpouring was the Day of Pentecost in Acts 2.

James 5:7-8 tells us that there is an early and latter rain before the Lord comes again. In farming, there must be an early rain to soak the ground for the seed to take root. Then there needs to be small rains after that. However, farmers know they have to have a big rain (a latter rain) to bring in a big harvest.

There have been revivals, awakenings, moves of God's Spirit over the centuries since the Day of Pentecost. We are now in the signs of the end times, and there is a great outpouring of God's Spirit that is beginning.

Every revival and every great awakening or move of God has been started with prayer and praise and worship. In times past, when prayer and worship became mechanical and not from a hungry, sensitive heart, the revival or awakening died.

Isaiah 60:1 indicates that God's glory, His supernatural miracles, will be seen. Young and old will flow together.

Those who have gone away from the Lord will return to Him. Many will be converted to the Lord in this hour.

Chapter 14

WHEN YOUR FAITH IS CHALLENGED

Because we live in a fallen world and there is an enemy who opposes us, there are times when our faith in God will be challenged. We have to determine ahead of time to have a fixed heart upon God's Word. We are living in what the Bible refers to as the last days, and the enemy has intensified his efforts to stop God's Kingdom from advancing before his time is up and he is removed from the earth.

Psalm 108:1 KJV says, **"O God, my heart is fixed; I will sing and give praise. . . ."** *The Modern English Version* of this verse says, **"O God, my heart is determined; I will sing and give praise with my whole heart."**

In times like these, we determine to fix our hearts upon the Lord and His Word. Why? Because it is the only true source of constant strength and help in time of need when our minds and emotions are being challenged.

When my late husband died, I wasn't expecting him to die. I expected him to live. He had always taught that we do not base our faith upon people's experiences, but we base our faith upon God's Word. I drew to God and His Word. I asked Him to give me what I needed from the Word of God. I heard the still small voice of the Holy Spirit speaking in my heart, and I knew I was to be with our church and speak into them as the Holy Spirit was speaking to me. I also knew I was to rise up and steady the ship, taking us forward.

I actually had a very unusual experience when my husband died as I worshipped God. I heard angels singing with me as I worshipped. However, when I began to sing a song that says, "Jesus, I believe in You; Jesus, I belong to You. You're the reason that I live, the reason that I say with all I am," the angels stopped singing.

I asked the Lord why they stopped. He said, "They can't sing your confession." (That song is a confession of your faith in Jesus still. This and other stories are in my book, *The Draw of Heaven.)*

Later, there were moments where I had tears of emotion, but I remember within the first few days the spirit of grief lifted from me. An unusual grace came upon my life that I cannot explain in natural terms. I still had moments where someone would say something touching that my husband had said or done that moved my tears, but then they would stop as I listened to their stories.

The Holy Spirit instructed me what I was to do week by week. Family and friends surrounded me, giving me support. We moved forward through God's grace. I remember as I praised and worshipped God, I was being healed along with others and receiving strength.

DAVID'S FAITH WAS CHALLENGED

Second Samuel 12:19-23 tells about when David had sinned with Bathsheba. (After her husband's death, David married her. However, she had already become pregnant.) When the baby was born, the baby was very sick. The prophet Nathan had said the child was going to die. However, David fasted and prayed for the child and said that possibly the child might live.

When the child died, <u>David arose to wash himself and went to the house of God to worship</u>. His servants around him were surprised. He told them when the child was alive, he fasted and prayed; but once the child had died, he told them, **"I shall go to him** [the child], **but he shall not return to me"** (v. 23). David knew the child would not be resurrected on earth, but would be raised to Heaven and one day he would see him again. David also knew he needed to worship and draw upon God's strength.

Strength can rise within us when we choose to worship God. Not only is it helpful to worship individually, but also we experience strength when we worship with others.

Worshipping with other believers strengthens our spirits to rise in the midst of difficult times. Like coals of a fire heaped together, we experience God's presence in a powerful restorative way when worshipping with others.

Chapter 15

THE WILL TO PRAISE AND WORSHIP – A MAJOR KEY TO YOUR VICTORIES!

Psalm 34:1,3 MEV states:

> I will bless the Lord at <u>all</u> times; His praise will <u>continually</u> be in my mouth . . . Oh magnify the Lord with me, and let us exalt His name together.

<u>The will to worship will get you into worship</u>. The Psalmist understood the power of his own will. This is why he says over and over:

> "I will praise the Lord." (Psalm 7:17; 9:1; 57:9; 71:22; 109:30; 118:28; 146:2.)

> "I will sing to the Lord." (Psalm 13:6; 57:7; 59:16; 61:8; 89:1; 104:33; 108:1,3.)

"I will bless the Lord." (Psalm 16:7; 63:4; 145:1-2.)

Praise and worship opens the door to God's presence and all that He is to us. He comes to inhabit the praises of His people. This means that His love, His mercy, His grace, His wisdom and counsel, His power, and His help – all come to us when we praise and worship Him.

Praise and worship is a key to victory in the Kingdom of God. Keys represent authority. When Jesus said in Matthew 16:19 that He was giving His disciples keys of Heaven's Kingdom, it was not just for those living at that time. Those keys are for us today as well.

Praise and worship is a key. That key unlocks the door of victory in our lives when we go through testing times. It requires faith to praise and worship when we go through testing times.

Praise lifts faith off of the ground like an airplane that has taxied on the runway and takes off. Praise enables God's people to rise up and stand against the enemy. Jesus said He would build His Church and the gates of hell would not prevail against His Church (Matthew 16:18). You and I are the Church, and part of the Church all around the world. Although we live in a fallen world and there are storms in life, we've been given victory to overcome.

Our faith in the victory of Jesus Christ over the devil is released in praise and worship, and Heaven is able to help us rise above the storms of life and keep standing. Psalm 107:29 AMP says, **"He hushed the storm to a gentle whisper, so that the waves of the sea were still."**

Romans 8:37-38 GW says this. Let's look at verse 38 first: **"I am convinced that nothing can separate us from God's love which Christ Jesus our Lord shows us."** Now let's look at verse 37: **"The One who loves us gives us an overwhelming victory in all these difficulties."**

Thank God that he gives us the victory through our Lord Jesus Christ.

1 Corinthians 15:57 GW

AUTHOR CONTACT

If you would like to contact Sharon Daugherty, find out more information, purchase books, or request her to speak, please contact:

Sharon Daugherty
Victory Christian Center, Inc.
7700 South Lewis Avenue
Tulsa, Oklahoma 74136-7700 U.S.A.
918-491-7700
www.victory.com
info@victory.com

Follow Sharon Daugherty!
twitter.com/DaughertySharon